First World War
and Army of Occupation
War Diary
France, Belgium and Germany

33 DIVISION
98 Infantry Brigade,
Brigade Machine Gun Company
and Brigade Trench Mortar Battery
16 October 1915 - 5 July 1916

WO95/2427/5-6

The Naval & Military Press Ltd
www.nmarchive.com
Published in association with The National Archives

Published by

The Naval & Military Press Ltd

Unit 10 Ridgewood Industrial Park,

Uckfield, East Sussex,

TN22 5QE England

Tel: +44 (0) 1825 749494

www.naval-military-press.com

www.nmarchive.com

This diary has been reprinted in facsimile from the original. Any imperfections are inevitably reproduced and the quality may fall short of modern type and cartographic standards.

© **Crown Copyright**
Images reproduced by permission of The National Archives, London, England, 2015.

Contents

Document type	Place/Title	Date From	Date To
Heading	WO95/2427-6 Brig. Trench Mortar By Oct-Dec 1915		
Heading	33 Div 98th Trench Mortar Bty Oct-Dec 1915		
Heading	3rd Army 98th Trench Mortar Battery Vol I Oct 15		
Heading	War Diary Of 98th Trench Mortar Battery from Oct 16th. 1915 to Oct 31.1915 Volume I		
War Diary	Valheureux	16/10/1915	16/10/1915
War Diary	Domarts	17/10/1915	20/10/1915
War Diary	Villers-Bretoneux	21/10/1915	22/10/1915
War Diary	Villers-Bocage	23/10/1915	31/10/1915
Heading	War Diary of 98th Trench Mortar Battery from Nov 1st 1915 to Nov 30th 1915 152 Bde Volume 2		
War Diary	Villers-Bocage	01/11/1915	05/11/1915
War Diary	Pont-Noyelles	06/11/1915	09/11/1915
War Diary	Aveluy	10/11/1915	27/11/1915
War Diary	Henencourt	28/11/1915	30/11/1915
Heading	War Diary of 95th Trench Mortar Battery from 1-12-15 to 31-12-15 Volume 3		
War Diary	Lavieville	01/12/1915	20/12/1915
War Diary	Aveluy	21/12/1915	31/12/1915
War Diary	Beuvry	01/07/1916	05/07/1916

WO 95 2427/6
BRIG. TRENCH MORTAR BY.
OCT-DEC 1915

~~51ST DIVISION~~ 33 DIV
~~152ND~~ INFY BDE

98

98TH TRENCH MORTAR BTY
OCT ~~NOV~~ - DEC 1915

26

151/7381

3rd Army

98th French Inf.n Batt.y

Vol I

Oct 15

Confidential

War Diary

of

98th Trench Mortar Battery

From Oct 16th 1915 to Oct 31. 1915

Volume I.

Army Form C. 2118.

WAR DIARY
or
INTELLIGENCE SUMMARY.
(Erase heading not required.)

98th Trench Mortar Battery

Instructions regarding War Diaries and Intelligence Summaries are contained in F. S. Regs., Part II. and the Staff Manual respectively. Title pages will be prepared in manuscript.

Place	Date	Hour	Summary of Events and Information	Remarks and references to Appendices
VALHEUREUX.	16-10-15	9.30 a.m.	Battery left in 2 motor lorries to report at the Hqrs of the 26th Division.	
		12.30 p.m.	Arrived at Hqrs of the 26th Division which was at VILLERS-BRETONNEUX and there we were told to report to Hqrs of 79th Inf Bgde at CACHY.	
		1. P.M.	Arrived at Hqrs of 79th Inf Bgde and from there we were sent to HOMARTS to our billets.	
		1.30 P.M.	Arrived at HOMARTS and were billeted. Billets were good; indented for Camp Kettle and Blankets. In the meantime we borrowed them from R.A.M.C. Weather fine throughout.	
HOMARTS.	17-10-15	9.30 – 12.30	Route March.	
		2. P.M.	Cleaning guns and spare parts. Afterwards went to Bgd Hqrs at CACHY to see about internal matters connected with the Battery. Weather fine.	
HOMARTS.	18-10-15	9.30 – 12.30	Gun drill and digging in the fields.	
		2. P.M.	Rifle inspection. Weather fine but cold.	
HOMARTS.	19-10-15	9.30 – 11.30	Route March.	
		2 p.m.	Cleaning guns and spare parts. Camp Kettle arrived, handed back borrowed ones to R.A.M.C. Weather cold and damp.	
HOMARTS.	20-10-15	9.30 – 12.30	Route March; at 1.45 received an order from Bgde Hqrs to be ready to move tomorrow; at 6 p.m. received an order to report at once to Trench Hqrs at VILLERS-BRETONNEUX. So marched off at once and reported at 9.30 p.m. billeted in some workshops. Blankets arrived before leaving HOMARTS. Weather fine, handed in borrowed Blankets to R.A.M.C.	

W Phipps 2Lt

Army Form C. 2118.

WAR DIARY
or
INTELLIGENCE SUMMARY.
(Erase heading not required.)

98th Trench Mortar Battery

Place	Date	Hour	Summary of Events and Information	Remarks and references to Appendices
VILLERS-BRETONNEUX	21-10-15	9.30 a.m.	Ordered to be ready to move at short notice as "Stood by" in billets all day. Received an order to the effect that a Motor Lorry would arrive at 6.30 am the next day to convey us to Hdqrs of 19th Inf Bgde at VILLERS-BOCAGE. Weather fine.	
		6.p.m.		
VILLERS-BRETONNEUX	22-10-15	8 am	Motor Lorry late; arrived at 8 a.m. guns on bits packed on it and an unloading party; remainder set out to hand. Route via AMIENS to VILLERS-BOCAGE. Lorry arrived at VILLERS-BOCAGE. Billets obtained. Remainder arrived at Villers VILLERS-BOCAGE. Weather fine but cold.	
		9.15 a.m		
		2.30 p.m		
VILLERS-BOCAGE	23-10-15	9.30	Payed the men; easy day after long march of the previous day. Gun and rifle inspection. Weather cold and dull but no rain.	
		2.p.m		
VILLERS-BOCAGE	24-10-15	9.30 a.m - 12.p.m.	Route hand. Weather dull and cold, at about 5.30 pm commenced to rain, continuing all through the night	
VILLERS-BOCAGE	25-10-15	9.30 - 12.30	Gun drill and digging in the beds Inspection by the G.O.C. Weather dull and very cold	
		3.30 p.m		
VILLERS-BOCAGE	26-10-15	9.30 - 12.30	Route hand. Clothing Inspection. Weather fine	
		2 p.m		

Army Form C. 2118

WAR DIARY
or
INTELLIGENCE SUMMARY.
(Erase heading not required.)

98th French Mortar Battery

Instructions regarding War Diaries and Intelligence Summaries are contained in F.S. Regs. Part II. and the Staff Manual respectively. Title pages will be prepared in manuscript.

Place	Date	Hour	Summary of Events and Information	Remarks and references to Appendices
VILLERS-BOCAGE	27-10-15	9·30 -12·30	Physical drill and gun drill in the morning	
		2.30 pm	Gun and rifle inspection. Weather wet.	
VILLERS-BOCAGE	28-10-15	9·30 - 11 am	Route March	
			Gun + rifle inspection. Weather wet, rain starting about 11·15 am.	
		2 pm	Gun Drill. 2nd Lt. Hoffer and 5 men ordered to proceed to Bus for instruction	
VILLERS-BOCAGE	29-10-15	9·30 -12·30	Route March	
		2 PM	Gun Drill. 2nd Lt. Hoffer and 5 men all ranks joined 10th Division	
			Weather fine but cold	
VILLERS-BOCAGE	30-10-15	9·30 -12·30	Route March	
		2 PM	Gun and Rifle inspection. Weather cold and damp.	
VILLERS-BOCAGE	31-10-15	8·30 -12·30	Route March	
		2 PM	Kit Inspection. Weather cold and wet.	

R. Hopkins 2nd Lt.

G.H.Q.
Confidential

War Diary
of
98th Trench Mortar Battery

From Novr 1st 1915 To. Novr 30th 1915

Volume 2.

Army Form C. 2118.

WAR DIARY
or
INTELLIGENCE SUMMARY.
(Erase heading not required.)

98th French Mortar Battery

Instructions regarding War Diaries and Intelligence Summaries are contained in F. S. Regs., Part II. and the Staff Manual respectively. Title pages will be prepared in manuscript.

Place	Date	Hour	Summary of Events and Information	Remarks and references to Appendices
VILLERS-BOCAGE	1-11-15	9.30-12.30	Route March	
		2 pm	Gun and Rifle Inspection. Weather dull & cold rain in the evening	
VILLERS-BOCAGE	2-11-15	9.30-12.30	Route March. 2nd Lt Kappe & 5 Men returned from 10th Divn	
		2 pm	Kit inspection. Weather Wet.	
VILLERS-BOCAGE	3-11-15	9.30-12.30	Route March. 2 New guns arrived from Railhead	
		2 pm	Gun & rifle inspection. Weather Fine	
VILLERS-BOCAGE	4-11-15	9.30-12.30	Route March	
		2 pm	Kit Inspection. Weather Fine but very cold	
VILLERS-BOCAGE	5-11-15	9 am	2 Motor Lorries arrived to convey to HdQrs 10th Corps at QUERRIEUX. Reported to Camp Commandant at QUERRIEUX and then moved on to our billets	W/Wrapper 2nd Lt T.N.B. convoy
		10 am	at PONT-NOYELLES. Weather Showery	
PONT-NOYELLES	6-11-15	9.30-12.30	Route March	
		2.30	Gun drill. Weather Fine but cold.	

Army Form C. 2118.

WAR DIARY
or
INTELLIGENCE SUMMARY.
(Erase heading not required.)

98" Trench Mortar Battery

Instructions regarding War Diaries and Intelligence Summaries are contained in F. S. Regs., Part II. and the Staff Manual respectively. Title pages will be prepared in manuscript.

Place	Date	Hour	Summary of Events and Information	Remarks and references to Appendices
PONT-NOYELLES	7-11-15	9.30 12.30	Route March. Kit Inspection. Weather fine but very cold.	
		2 pm		
PONT-NOYELLES	8-11-15	9.30 -12.30	Drawing ammunition and Route March. Weather fine	
		2 pm	Gun drill. Weather fine	
PONT-NOYELLES	9-11-15	10 am	Left for Hdqrs of 153rd Inft Bgd.	
		11.30 am	arrived at Headquarters 153rd Bgd at AVELUY via ALBERT and were billeted there. Weather showery.	
AVELUY	10-11-15	9 am 3 pm	In the trenches selecting gun positions. Weather wet. Trenches in a disgusting state, mud up to the knees in places	
AVELUY	11-11-15	9 am 2 pm	In the trenches selecting gun positions and observation posts. Great difficulty arising out of lack of telephone, but eventually obtained suitable position. Weather wet and windy.	
AVELUY.	12-11-15	9 am -3.30	Digging in the gun Weather wet	
AVELUY	13-11-15		Further improvement to gun position. Weather fine.	[signature] 98" T.M.B. 4/11/15

#353 Wt. W3541/1454 700,000 5/15 D. D. & L. A.D.S.S./Forms/C. 2118.

Army Form C. 2118.

WAR DIARY
or
INTELLIGENCE SUMMARY.
(Erase heading not required.)

98" Trench Mortar Battery

Place	Date	Hour	Summary of Events and Information	Remarks and references to Appendices
AVELUY	14-11-15		Improving gun positions. Weather fine	
AVELUY	15-11-15		General work in the trenches repairing approaches to emplacements. Gun inspection. Weather fine but cold. Snow fell during the night	
AVELUY	16-11-15	9:30 – 4:30	Commenced new bomb proof dug out for the gun teams in the trenches. Weather fine but cold. Snow again falling at night	
AVELUY	17-11-15	9:30 – 4:30	Working on dug out	
		11 noon	Fired 4. 13.16 bombs at new German earthwork. (X.7.B.88) Trench Map sheet 57 D. S.E 4) 2 went into German trench, one on parapet and one a "dud" exploded. Weather fine & cold	
AVELUY	18-11-15	9:30 a.m – 4:30 p.m	Working on dug out. Gun inspection	
		5 p.m.	Weather fine but cold	
AVELUY	19-11-15	9:30 – 4:30	Working on dug out and repaired bed which had sunk. Weather fine but cold. Trenches gradually drying up.	
AVELUY	20-11-15	9:30 – 4:30	Working on dug out.	
		11:30 a.m	Two light (old) bombs at German earthwork (X.7.B.88) Trench Map sheet 57 D.S.E 4 which had been repaired after our firing 17-11-15. One bomb exploded. Weather fine but cold.	[signature] O.C. T.M.B.

Army Form C. 2118.

WAR DIARY
or
INTELLIGENCE SUMMARY.
(Erase heading not required.)

98th French Motor Tractor Battery

Instructions regarding War Diaries and Intelligence Summaries are contained in F. S. Regs., Part II. and the Staff Manual respectively. Title pages will be prepared in manuscript.

Place	Date	Hour	Summary of Events and Information	Remarks and references to Appendices
AVELUY	21-11-15	9.30 – 4.30	Working on dug out. Weather fine and cold.	
AVELUY	22-11-15	9.30 – 4.30	Working on dug out, gun and spent part inspection. Weather cold and foggy	
AVELUY	23-11-15	9.30 – 4.30	Working on dug out. Weather cold and foggy	
AVELUY	24-11-15	9.30 – 4.30	Working on dug out. Weather fine but cold	
AVELUY	25-11-15	9.30 – 4.30	Working on dug out and Commenced another trench proof dug out. O.C. Battery went to School of Motors taking 3 bombs complete with charges and fuses to test condition after being in the trenches result two fired and one failed. Weather fine	
AVELUY	26-11-15	9.30 – 4.30 1pm	Working on the dug outs. Fired 6 18lb bombs on the German trench (X7387 Sheet 57d SE 4) 3 burst and 3 did. Weather fine but very cold	R.H. Murphy 2nd Lt. H.T.M.B. Comdg. 98

Army Form C. 2118.

WAR DIARY
or
INTELLIGENCE SUMMARY.

(Erase heading not required.)

98th Trench Howitzer Battery

Place	Date	Hour	Summary of Events and Information	Remarks and references to Appendices
AVELUY	27-11-15	8-11.30	Dug out the gun pits and withdrew all stores from the trenches	
		4. p.m.	Allotted 2 G.S. waggons and number to next billets at HENENCOURT	
		6. p.m.	Arrived at HENENCOURT received Billets. Weather fine and cold	
HENENCOURT	28-11-15		Morning spent cleaning billets which had been handed over to us in a filthy state. Reconnoitred trench Mortar Officer came over and arranged a place to build a range for the purpose of firing dummy bombs. Weather cold, a clear frosty day.	
HENENCOURT	29-11-15		Stand-bye in billets awaiting orders. Weather wet.	
HENENCOURT	30-11-15	9 a.m.	Received an order to proceed to LAVEVILLE	
		2 p.m.	proceeded to LAVEVILLE	
		3 p.m.	Arrived at LAVEVILLE received billets. Quite satisfactory except no drinking water can be obtained in the village, and no meals can be attached to battery; arranged with 2 Lahore Batt. to share water. Weather Fine	

E Knapp. 2/L
Comdg 98 TMB

51

G.H.Q.

Confidential

War Diary

of

98th French Trench Mortar Battery

From 1-12-15 To 31-12-15

Volume 3.

12/
7932

Army Form C. 2118.

WAR DIARY
or
INTELLIGENCE SUMMARY.
(Erase heading not required.)

98th Second Porlac Battery

Place	Date	Hour	Summary of Events and Information	Remarks and references to Appendices
LAVIEVILLE	1-12-15	10-11.30	Route March. Looked for a suitable place to dig gun emplacement	
		2.30	Gun and rifle inspection. Weather Wet.	
LAVIEVILLE	2-12-15	9.30-12.30	Route March	
		2.30-4pm	Commenced to dig gun emplacement. Weather dull and cloudy but no rain fell	
LAVIEVILLE	3-12-15	10-12	Route March	
		2pm	Gun and rifle inspection. Weather Wet	
LAVIEVILLE	4-12-15	10-11	Route March	
		11am	Pay Parade and Kit inspection	
		2pm	Issue of new clothes. Weather Wet	
LAVIEVILLE	5-12-15	9.30-12.30	Digging gun emplacement	
		2.30pm	Gun and rifle inspection. Weather showers	
LAVIEVILLE	6-12-15	9.30-12.30	Digging gun emplacement	
		2pm	Gun and rifle inspection. Weather rain at intervals windy	

WAR DIARY
or
INTELLIGENCE SUMMARY.
(Erase heading not required.)

Army Form C. 2118.

98th Trench Mortar Battery

Place	Date	Hour	Summary of Events and Information	Remarks and references to Appendices
LAVIEVILLE	7-12-15	9.30 - 10.30	Digging gun emplacement	
		2.30 pm	Lecture on the use of gas helmet. Gas drill & inspection of gas helmets. Weather showery, wet night	
LAVIEVILLE	8-12-15	9.30 - 12.30	Working on gun emplacement	
		8.30	Bathing parade. Weather fine.	
LAVIEVILLE	9-12-15	9.30 - 11.30	Route March in Toonery	
		2.30 pm	Gun and rifle inspection. Weather wet	
LAVIEVILLE	10-12-15	9.30 - 12	Route March	
		2.30 pm	Kit Inspection. Weather Wet.	
LAVIEVILLE	11-12-15	9.30 - 11.30	Route March	
		2.30	Gun & rifle Inspection	
		7 pm	48 rounds of heavy bombs complete arrived 24 New fuses & 24 old fuses. Pattern. Weather Wet	
LAVIEVILLE	12-12-15	9.30 - 12.30	Route March	
		2.30	Gun and spare part inspection. Weather dull but no rain fell	

Army Form C. 2118.

Duplicate

WAR DIARY
or
INTELLIGENCE SUMMARY.

(Erase heading not required)

98th Trench Mortar Battery

Instructions regarding War Diaries and Intelligence Summaries are contained in F. S. Regs. Part II. and the Staff Manual respectively. Title pages will be prepared in manuscript.

Place	Date	Hour	Summary of Events and Information	Remarks and references to Appendices
LAVIEVILLE	13-12-15	9.30 – 12.30	Further work on gun emplacement and commenced a new emplacement. Weather fine and frosty.	
		2.30	Gun and rifle inspection.	
LAVIEVILLE	14-12-15	9.30 – 12.30	Working on gun emplacements fitting overhead cover.	
		2.30 – 4	ditto. Weather fine and frosty.	
LAVIEVILLE	15-12-15	8.30 – 10 am	Finished off emplacement. Fired 4 shots (Heavy lumps) experimenting with new fuze, all good bursts.	
		2.30 pm	Route march. Weather frosty and damp.	
LAVIEVILLE	16-12-15	9.30 – 12.30	Route march. The O.C. Battery went to School of Mortars III Army to obtain a few details about new fuze. Weather showery.	
LAVIEVILLE	17-12-15	9.30 – 12.30	Working on gun emplacement.	
		2.30	Paying out. Weather fine.	
LAVIEVILLE	18-12-15	9.30 – 12.30	Route March.	
		2.30	Gun and rifle inspection. Weather fine.	
LAVIEVILLE	19-12-15	11.45 am	Fired 6 Heavy lumps at gun emplacement which we dug under & supervision of G.O.C. 51st Division previously.	
		2.30 pm	Gun inspection. Weather fine.	

WAR DIARY or INTELLIGENCE SUMMARY

Army Form C. 2118.

98th Trench Mortar Battery

Place	Date	Hour	Summary of Events and Information	Remarks and references to Appendices
LAVIEVILLE	20-12-15	11 am	Left LAVIEVILLE to proceed to AVELUY	
		12.30	Arrived at AVELUY. Received billets. Weather dull but no rainfall	
AVELUY	21-12-15	6-8	Selecting gun positions and bringing guns & beds into the trenches	
		8.30-1pm	Digging in	
		2.30pm	Fired 2 Heavy bombs at X.I.A.6.7. Trench Map 57D S.E.4. for ranging purposes, both burst. Weather misty & wet	
AVELUY	22-12-15	9-12	Endeavouring to drain under Trm gun emplacements	
		2.30pm	Fired 6 heavy bombs (2 blind) at X.I.A.6.7 Trench Map 57D S.E.4 damaged to German parapet considerable, arranged with Infantry to have machine gun trained on gap. Weather misty & wet	
AVELUY	23-12-15		Selecting New gun emplacements, repairing dugout. Weather showery	
AVELUY	24-12-15	1.30pm	Commenced New gun emplacement. One gun fired by shell fire	
		4pm	Dug gun out and found it had sustained no damage. Weather wet	
AVELUY	25-12-15		Quiet Day. Guns and gun positions inspected. Weather showery	

WAR DIARY
or
INTELLIGENCE SUMMARY.

(Erase heading not required.)

90th Trench Howitzer Battery

Place	Date	Hour	Summary of Events and Information	Remarks and references to Appendices
AVELUY	26-12-15	2.15 pm	Completed New gun Emplacement. Fired 1 Heavy Round for ranging purposes. Weather dull, rained heavily during the night.	
AVELUY	27-12-15		Improving approaches to Gun Emplacement. Weather dull but no rain fell.	
AVELUY	28-12-15	3.30 pm	Went over & tested the trunks which we have had order to move into on Jan 2. 1916. Gun and rifle inspection. Weather fine.	
AVELUY	29-12-15	11.45 am	Fired 1 Heavy bomb on X.1.A.6.8. Trench Map 57D.S.E⁰. It burst in German parapet and 2 machine guns fired a gap made at night. Enemy discovered our gun position and shelled it with light artillery but did no damage to gun or gun bed. Weather fine	
AVELUY	30-12-15	12 midnight	Repaired one gun position which had sunk owing to the wet. Fired 4 light bombs at X.1.A.6.5. 66. 67.68. Trench Map 57D. S.E⁰. all burst well, 3 landed on a parapet and 1. into the trench: Reveration caused by very mild. Snow. enemy's flares also helped us in ranging. Weather fine.	
AVELUY	31-12-15		Further work on gun position. Weather showery.	

Wh Mappin 2nd Lt
Comdg 90 T.M.B.

T.M. 33 July

Army Form C. 2118.

WAR DIARY
of 98th TRENCH MORTAR BATTERY
INTELLIGENCE SUMMARY
(Erase heading not required.)

Vol 1

Place	Date	Hour	Summary of Events and Information	Remarks and references to Appendices
BEUVRY	1916 July 1		Battery in Rest Billets. Training carried out with Class attacks for tomorrow. Casualties - Nil.	CSi
	2		Left-Half Battery proceeded to GIVENCHY Left Sub section to relieve 19th T.M. Bty. of continuous practice Training. Casualties - Nil	CSi
			Right Half Battery and Class of instruction coach Training. Casualties - Nil	
	3		Right Half Battery relieved Left Battery of 100th T.M. Bty. in GIVENCHY Right Sub section. 1 Officer & 92nd T.M.Bty. Headqrs are command of Left 1/2 of 100th T.M.B. in GIVENCHY Left Sub section. O.C. Bty. visits GIVENCHY Left. Casualties - Nil	CSi
	4		Half Battery in position as above O.C. Bty visits GIVENCHY Section. Casualties - Nil	CSi
	5		Left Half Battery in action in support of raid by units of 19th (Div) Bde on salient of this Sec. Assaulter Officer 1. O.R. 2	CSi